Life in a Medieval Village

Gwyneth Morgan

Published in cooperation with Cambridge University Press
Lerner Publications Company, Minneapolis

Editors' Note: In preparing this edition of *The Cambridge Topic Books* for publication, the editors have made only a few minor changes in the original material. In some isolated cases, British spelling and usage were altered in order to avoid possible confusion for our readers. Whenever necessary, information was added to clarify references to people, places, and events in British history. An index was also provided in each volume.

Morgan, Gwyneth.
    Life in a medieval village.

    (A Cambridge topic book)
    Includes index.
    Summary: Describes the various aspects of life in a thirteenth century English village including housing, food, dress, occupations, laws, role of the church, and the activities of the serfs, farmers, and the lord and lady of the manor.
    1. England—Social life and customs—Medieval period, 1066-1485—Juvenile literature. [1. England—Social life and customs—Medieval period, 1066-1485. 2. Middle Ages—Social life and customs]
    I. Title.
    DA185.M67 1982   942'.009732   81-13735
    ISBN 0-8225-1207-6 (lib. bdg.)   AACR2

This edition first published 1982 by Lerner Publications Company by permission of Cambridge University Press.

Original edition copyright © 1975 by Cambridge University Press as part of *The Cambridge Introduction to the History of Mankind: Topic Book.*

International Standard Book Number: 0-8225-1207-6
Library of Congress Catalog Card Number: 81-13735

Manufactured in the United States of America

This edition is available exclusively from:
Lerner Publications Company, 241 First Avenue North, Minneapolis, Minnesota 55401

1 2 3 4 5 6 7 8 9 10 86 85 84 83 82

Contents

The lord and lady of the manor are shown in this illustration from a thirteenth-century book.

1 THE PEASANT AND HIS HOME

The village

The village described in this book is equal to one 'knight's fee', that is, an estate rich enough to support one knight to serve the king when required. The King is Henry III of England, and the year is 1265. There is a lord of the manor, Robert Fitzralph, who lives in the manor house and holds his lands, as a subtenant, from a rich local abbey. He pays the abbot a fixed money rent every Easter and Michaelmas (29 September). His grandfather actually served as a knight but his father agreed with the abbot to pay a cash rent instead, and this has been passed on to the present lord.

The whole village has about two hundred inhabitants and all the tenants, free and unfree, rent their land from Lord Robert. They do him service or pay him rent according to the terms of their lease. All of them have to do some work, but the free peasants pay most of their dues in money or produce, and, instead of doing specific jobs, buy him special luxuries like pepper (worth 12*d* a pound in the early thirteenth century) or spices. The unfree tenants, or 'serfs', work for him without pay and pay their rent partly in money or in produce, but mainly with the work they do. Landlords and tenants are bound to one another by personal and feudal obligations.

As you can see, the two most important buildings in the village are the church and the manor house with its barns and yards. The church is the only stone building. The manor house has stone foundations below a solid structure of wood, wattle and plaster. The villagers' cottages and the priest's house are also made of wood and plaster and vary in size according to the wealth and status of the tenants. As this is a midland village, the settlement is surrounded by three huge common fields divided into strips. In the common pastures beyond, the villagers can turn their animals out to graze at certain times of the year. The woods and scrubland belong to Lord Robert and the forest comes under the king's law.

A medieval village (Middle Ditchford, Gloucestershire) that was deserted late in the Middle Ages, when sheep farming replaced corn. From photographs like this we can trace the layout of a village clearly; the strips in the fields can still be seen from the air. The irregular plots in the centre of the photograph are the sites of the peasants' cottages and gardens. Compare with the modern artist's drawing opposite.

5

The free peasant

To see what life in the village is like, we will follow the life of one of the richer freemen, John, son of Alfred. He lives in one of the larger cottages near the church, with his wife, Alice, and his two sons, John the younger (sometimes called 'John, grandson of Alfred'), and Lambert. John rents certain strips of land in the common fields and his cottage and garden from Lord Robert. He pays a cash rent four times a year, gives his lord one pound of the aromatic spice cummin and a pair of spurs at Michaelmas and Christmas (worth 6½d), and does certain duties which are compulsory for all tenants.

King

Cash rent

Lord of the manor
(sub-tenant)

Abbot
(chief tenant)

Cash rent for
knight's fee

Labour, cash, goods
and services

Serfs

Cash, goods and services

John, a freeman

William son of Edwin, free	*s*	*d*
Rent	7	3
2 doz. eggs at Easter		½
1 hen at Easter		1
3 days carting yearly, at 1½*d* per day		4½
1 piglet yearly		½
Total rent per year	7	9½

Edward son of Roger, unfree	*s*	*d*
Cash	2	3
2 works per week, at ½*d* each, from Michaelmas to Nativity of St John the Baptist (38 weeks)	3	2
Harrowing 1 acre at sowing time		2
2 days ploughing, at 2*d* per day		4
2 days digging vineyard, at 1½*d* per day		3
4 days hay making, at 2*d* per day		8
3 days shearing, at ½*d* per day		1½
4 days harvesting, at 1½*d* per day		6
4 days threshing, at 1*d* per day		4
Total rent per year	7	9½

As part of his duty as a tenant, John has to help mend the road that runs through the village. Like most lords, Robert Fitzralph does not take much interest in the work and thinks it a great nuisance and expense and waste of time. But since the sheriff's horse stumbled in a rut a few years back, and the sheriff hurt his arm and lost his temper, the lord feels obliged to do something about repairing the worst parts of the road each autumn. All the tenants are pressed into service to quarry and cut the stones and to fill up the holes and ruts.

Some dues cannot be exchanged for money, even by freemen, and these have been fixed by local custom for generations. John must give his lord a hen, worth 1*d*, at Christmas and a basket of eggs at Easter. When he dies Alice or his eldest son will be obliged to give his best animal to the lord. This gift is called a 'heriot' and has to be paid before a son can succeed to his father's holding.

Apart from these dues, John enjoys far more personal freedom than his unfree neighbours. He and his family are personally free, and can move away from the village if they want to go and serve another lord or to live in the town. There is no danger that they will be sent to another estate or sold, like serfs. Then, John can own and carry weapons, according to his income and status. King Henry II made it compulsory for all freemen to have some kind of weapon, varying from a sword or spear for the poorest to a complete suit of mail, with a shield and horse, for a wealthy knight or noble. (When a serf is set free, his lord gives him a weapon as a symbol of his new status.) At the moment John has only a sword, given to him by his grandfather who fought in the Crusades. If he gets richer, he will have to buy a helmet and shield as well.

Perhaps the greatest advantage of freedom is being able to buy or acquire land of one's own. John might lease a small piece of land from one of his neighbours for a nominal rent (for example, 3*d* at Whitsuntide and Martinmas; a pair of gloves or ½*d* at Easter, or some spices) or, with his lord's con- sent, he could reclaim some uncultivated land for himself. In the thirteenth century it is quite common for enterprising and energetic freemen to get permission from their lords to clear scrub and woodland to grow their own crops and the profits are entirely their own, except that they will have to pay a penny or two as rent to the lord. This newly developed land, or 'assart', can be very valuable to John, for he can sell the crops he grows there and use the money to buy better farm-tools, more animals or luxuries for his family.

Like an increasing number of his class, John can read and write. As a boy he found his lessons very difficult, and the local parish priest thought he was slow and unwilling, but now he realises it was worth all the effort. Sometimes he can be useful to the royal sheriffs and justices, too. As communications are so poor, the king finds it very difficult to get hold of facts and figures about land-holders, taxes, incomes, services due to the crown and so on, and the best way to get information (as William I's 'Domesday' enquiry showed in 1086) is to send the royal clerks round to each county, where

A fourteenth-century cottage in Hagbourne, Berkshire, with a cruck structure. The little shed under the eave at the left is a much later addition.

they send for the lord, the parish priest and the most trustworthy and sensible tenants from each village in it and question them. They have to swear solemnly to tell the truth and can be punished for lying or for concealing useful information.

John's home

John's cottage is one of the biggest in the village, and stands in a large garden with fruit trees, a vegetable patch and beehives. Alice has a small flower garden, where she grows sweet-smelling flowers, like lavender, and herbs to be used for cooking and preserving.

How it was built

John built the cottage himself, with the help of his kinsman, the village carpenter, and the thatcher from the next village. As stone is expensive to quarry, cut and transport, it is made out of materials available locally – strong branches and trunks of trees on the assart; twigs and thinner branches from the nearby woods and common land, and clay from a claypit near the village.

The frame at each end of the cottage is made of two very strong thick branches of oak propped in a triangle-shape. This shape is called a 'cruck' and so the cottages built in this pattern are known as 'cruck cottages'. The base of each branch is fixed tightly into holes in the ground and earth and stones are packed tight round them and banged down hard. Two of these 'cruck' frames are set far enough apart to form the two end walls of the cottage and two more are put up between them, so that the building is made up of three 'bays' or spaces between the crucks. Each space is about 12 feet (4 metres) long. Long, straight trimmed branches are laid along the top to form the main rafter and then other branches used to make the side frames.

When the framework of the cottage was ready, Alice and the two boys filled in the gaps between the posts and beams with 'wattle and daub' – thinner branches interwoven with pliable twigs (like willow), reeds and grass, and plastered with mud or clay to keep out the wind. The whole building was thatched by the thatcher, who cut reeds from the riverside and mixed them with straw before pegging and tying them firmly to the roof.

In spite of all the family's efforts, the cottage is not particularly strong or weatherproof and there is a constant danger of fire.

Inside the cottage

Inside the cottage are two rooms. The smaller has only one bay and a loft above. It is used for a storeroom and stable, where John keeps his oxen, his wife's chickens, and occasionally his pigs. He stores hay, grain, and fruit in the loft. On the ground floor he keeps barrels of beer, tubs of salted fish (for Lent) and salted meat, a few leather buckets, some small wooden barrels or 'tuns' and all his farm-tools, as well as some thick leather gloves and the horn he wears in his belt when he is out on the land.

The larger room is where the family live, eat and sleep. It is warmed by a fire in the centre of the room; there is no chimney and the smoke escapes through a hole in the roof. The fire is also for cooking and for light. There is very little furniture and it is very plain and simple: three-legged stools, a trestle table (made up of flat top and two sets of legs, which can be taken down and put away after meals) and two large wooden chests. There are no beds; at night the family bring out mattresses stuffed with straw and put them near the fire and cover themselves with coarse linen sheets and sheepskins for warmth. The sheets are a great luxury; most poor families have only very rough woollen blankets or just animal skins for bed-covers.

Sheets, skins and clothes are kept in the larger of the two chests. The smaller contains some of John's most precious possessions – six pewter plates and spoons and two brass pots. These are brought out only on very special occasions. Generally, Alice uses wooden spoons and pottery bowls. Her pestle and mortar (for grinding and crushing herbs, etc.) are made of wood, and her great stewpot or cauldron is iron.

John and his family eat very simple food. They cannot afford to buy imported wine and sugar and spices, nor can they afford meat very often. The few animals they keep are used mostly for farm work and are not bred for meat. Though a few oxen, cows and sheep are killed off in the autumn and the meat salted, it is because they cost too much to feed during the winter. The most usual meat for a peasant family comes from pigs, as smoked ham or bacon. Even when it is preserved in salt, the meat does not keep fresh for very long and often the bad taste has to be disguised by onion or garlic sauces. Fish is a rare treat, too, because the lord does not allow fishing in the river, and sea fish, also preserved in salt, are expensive. John does sometimes buy salted herrings or eels during Lent but generally he and Alice and the boys live off rye bread and vegetable stews made from onions, garlic, peas, beans, lentils and cabbage. Their protein comes from goat's or ewe's milk cheese. They drink milk, ale made from barley or mead from honey.

John grows most of his own fruit and vegetables in the garden round the cottage and he also keeps bees there. He tends them very carefully for they are valuable; honey is the common means of sweetening food.

This picture of bees and hives was painted in about 1200, in a 'bestiary' or book about animals, birds and insects. The hives are dome-shaped and made of plaited straw. John has five or six hives and is very proud of them. The bees find their pollen in the fruit-tree blossom and in the heather and gorse on the common land.

In the bitterly cold winter, this man is glad to come home to his warm cottage and thaw his toes by the fire. The iron pot stands on the hearth-stones and his wife has hung up the carcass of the pig he killed to smoke over the fire. She has also made sausages, as we can see.

An iron cauldron and earthenware jugs (*below*). The cauldron would hang over the fire with a chain through its handles or stand on its legs on the hearth stone. The jugs, probably home-made, were used for milk, beer or water. The simple decorations were made by scratching patterns on with a stick or by making thumb-prints in the wet clay. All these utensils were made in the thirteenth century in East Anglia.

The peasants' strips are still clearly visible in this photograph of fields at South Newington, Oxfordshire.

Daily work on the land

Nearly all the men, both free and unfree, spend most of their time working in the common fields growing crops for food. Every year, one of the fields is sown with wheat or rye for bread, another with barley for beer and some oats for the horses, while the third lies fallow. The fallow field is not sown at all, but is given a year's rest; the village animals graze on it and fertilise it with their manure.

The fields are divided into long narrow strips. Each one is a furlong in length (for that is the distance an ox team can plough before resting), but they are usually only about 20–24 feet (7 or 8 metres) wide. Each tenant has his own strips, all separate and scattered over the fields. His strips are equally divided between the three fields, so that he has a third of them growing wheat or rye, a third of them growing barley and oats, and a third of them fallow each year.

As a freeman, John works almost entirely on his own strips, and is generally very busy because he has more land than most of his neighbours. The work follows a regular pattern according to the seasons.

The autumn

John's working year begins in the autumn, after all the harvest has been carted home. His first job is to plough his strips in the field which has been lying fallow. He has ploughed them several times already in the summer, to get them well cultivated and to kill the weeds. Now he ploughs them again, and sows them with wheat or rye for next year's harvest, so that the young corn plants will come up and get well rooted before winter sets in. He sows the seed corn by hand, throwing it so that it falls into the furrows which the plough has made. Then he harrows the land flat to cover up the seed.

John ploughs with a team of oxen because they are strong and tough and cost less to feed than horses, though they are slower. The oxen are yoked together with wooden yokes and harnessed to a heavy plough. The plough has an iron coulter, like a big knife sticking down into the soil, to cut

12

This model of a very simple kind of plough is based on a thirteenth-century drawing. Another plough, more like the one described below, can be seen on the front of the book.

above right: Threshing with a 'flail', which has a wooden handle and a beater joined in the middle with a thong.

the furrow away at the side; then an iron share, like a tri-angular knife, which cuts it away from the soil underneath it; and then a curved wooden mould-board or breast behind the share, which turns it right over so that it lies upside down.

John sometimes ploughs with a team of two beasts, but sometimes he needs as many as six or eight. Then he has to borrow some from his neighbours or from the lord, for he only has two or three himself.

Next John ploughs his strips in the field which grew wheat and rye last year. This will grow barley and oats next year, but he does not sow it yet. Instead, he lets it lie rough, in great clods, as the plough has left it, all through the winter, so that the frost can freeze it right through. Then each tiny drop of water inside it will turn into ice and swell, so that it cracks up

the hard soil around it, and as soon as the thaw comes the clods will crumble down into a soft level seed bed for sowing with corn. In this way John makes the frost do the work of cultivating the soil for him.

But John does not spend all his time ploughing. Every week, all through the autumn and winter, he threshes out some of his grain from last year's harvest. He uses a flail, which has a heavy wooden striking piece 2 inches (5 centimetres) thick and 2 or 3 feet (80–100 centimetres) long, hinged with eel-skin to an even longer handle. He spreads out the sheaves of corn on the wooden floor of the barn, and whacks them as hard as he can with the flail, to knock the grain out of the ears. Then he forks up the straw and spreads it in the cattle yard. After that he opens the big doors on both sides of the barn to let the wind blow through. He gathers up the corn and bits of husk in a big shallow basket, and winnows it, throwing it up in the air so that the bits of husk blow away, and the corn, because it is heavier, falls back on to the barn floor. This is how he gets rid of the rubbish mixed up with the corn. Winnowing is quite light work, but threshing is terribly hard and exhausting, and it takes a strong man to do it.

13

The shepherd carries a strong wooden staff and wears warm clothes suitable for staying outside during the cold nights. Notice the bell worn round the neck of one of the sheep.

Some of the tools John uses and stores in his stable. Most of them were passed on from his father but the scythe is newly made by the village smith.

The winter

In November, the villagers turn their pigs out on to the common land and into the woods to fatten them up for the winter. Pigs love acorns and enjoy rooting around for them in the undergrowth. Most of them are killed off in December and salted, though some are kept for breeding next year. Alice finds cutting and salting the carcasses a most unpleasant task so John helps her when he has time. They store the salted joints in barrels and hang some of the legs over the cottage fire to make smoked hams. A few cows are killed and salted, too, but some have to be kept alive for breeding in the spring. By Christmas most of the winter food is ready and stored, and, apart from the salt-fish, they should have all they need.

After Christmas, John and his elder son spend a lot of their time in repairing the fences round the assart land and attending to the hedges which have grown too high, and too thin at the bottom, so that animals can get through. They cut out a lot of the hedge-wood, and lay the rest flat, but still joined to its roots, fixing it with stakes, so that the hedge is lower but much thicker; and in the spring, when the branches which have been laid flat send out new shoots, it will be thicker still. With the lord's permission, John can take away the branches and brushwood which have been cut out to use for firewood.

A little later on, John sometimes helps the lord's shepherd with the lambing, when the lambs are born in the grassfields and brought back with their mothers to be kept warm in the lord's sheepfold. For this, of course, John gets paid.

So long as the mild weather continues, as it sometimes does after Christmas, ploughing can go on, and John may begin to plough his strips in the third field, which was barley and oats last summer and will be fallow next summer. But when the frost and snow set in, no more ploughing can be done. John hates the cold, because work outside becomes arduous and miserable, and he is always wet and shivering. Sometimes in January and February he cannot work outside at all. Then he stays at home and mends his tools and helps Alice with the brewing and weaving; and of course there is always plenty of threshing to be done in the barn.

Towards the end of winter life can be very hard, especially if all the salt meat has been used up, and there is only bread and cheese to eat. Besides, if last year's harvest was a bad one, even bread may be short, and John and his family must be careful not to bake and eat too much of it in case the wheat and rye to make it from should run out before the next harvest comes.

The spring

John begins to feel happier when spring arrives and the weather gets warmer, and he can go out in the fields without layers of extra clothes and a sheepskin cape to keep out the cold. Now, too, there is more food for the cattle to eat, because the fresh grass begins to grow; and by April there is more food for John and his family as well, because the cows and ewes and goats, which have had a hard time all the winter, get more food and grow stronger, giving much more milk. From this time on, all through the spring and early summer, Alice can make large supplies of butter and cheese for her family.

As soon as the frost goes and the land dries a bit, John gets on with more ploughing. In the field which is to grow barley and oats he ploughs his strips again, and then in March or April, according to whether spring has come early or late, he sows them and harrows the seed in just as he did with his wheat and rye. Perhaps, too, he sows one or two of his strips in this field with peas and beans.

John's tools

These pictures come from a fourteenth-century calendar.

A flail for threshing corn. This shows the joint clearly.

The spade is wooden and has an iron rim all around the blade part to make digging easier. It has only one side for the digger to put his foot on (see also page 18).

For a job like weeding he needs strong leather gloves.

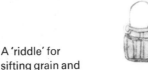

A 'riddle' for sifting grain and chaff.

The weeding crotch and hook are for clearing waste and overgrown land, or nasty weeds like thistles. John holds the plant with the forked or 'crotched' stick and cuts it with the other.

The wooden bucket has an iron handle, and possibly iron bands around it as well.

John uses a bill hook to trim hedges.

To cut the corn he needs a sickle.

For hay or long grass, a scythe.

The bill hook, sickle and scythe all have iron blades and wooden handles.

The man carries the seed in a straw or wicker basket round his neck on a cloth or a leather strap, and scatters the seed by hand. Often he takes a boy with him and a dog to scare away the birds, who swoop down and try to eat the corn.

The summer

All through the summer there is a lot of work to be done in the fields. While the corn is still young John spends a great deal of his time in weeding it, and Alice and Lambert help him. Whenever he can find the time, he gets on with the summer ploughing of his strips in the fallow field, ploughing in the weeds and killing them. By the end of the summer he hopes to be rid of all the weeds.

June begins the busiest season of the year. First comes hay harvest. John mows the long juicy grass in his strips of meadow by the river with a scythe (see above). He has to be careful, because he keeps the blade of the scythe very sharp. When the grass has been cut, John gets Alice and all the family to help. They fork it up into little haycocks, turning the haycocks over two or three times a day, so that the grass dries quickly in the sun and turns into hay while the nourishment for cattle is still in it. Then they load it on to a cart and take it home to make into a haystack, to be used all through next winter as the cattle need it.

In July and August comes the corn harvest. John cuts his barley and oats, and wheat and rye with a sickle, which has a curved steel blade on a short wooden handle. The blade has a saw-toothed edge. John puts his left arm around as much standing corn as he can manage and squeezes it up together. In his right hand he has his sickle, and he puts its curved blade round the stems of the corn, and then draws it sharply towards him so that the saw teeth cut the stems one by one till they are all cut through. Then Alice takes the corn and binds it up into a sheaf, with a band which she twists out of straw. After that the boys stand the sheaves up, leaning them together in stooks, or 'shocks' as some people call them, to dry in the wind and sun and finish their ripening. When the corn is all dry and ripe the sheaves are carted home to be made into a stack, and the stack is thatched with straw to keep out the rain. Later on, John will take the sheaves out of the stack, a few at a time, and gradually thresh out his corn through the next winter as he did through the last one.

The corn must not be carted home before it is thoroughly dry, or it will go bad in the stack. If the weather is fine and sunny at harvest time, John and all his family will have to work very hard in the fields, from six o'clock in the morning or even earlier, all through the day as long as the daylight lasts. Alice will bring out bread and cheese and beer at noon and in the evening for them to eat in the harvest field, so that they can get all the corn harvested quickly and stacked in good condition. But they will not mind how hard they work, because they know that if the weather is fine and the harvest is got in quickly it is going to be a good one and there will be plenty to eat all through the winter. What they hate is a wet harvest, when they can't get the corn cut and shocked, ripened

A man is harvesting with a sickle (you can see the teeth on the blade), while his wife gathers the cut corn. The lord's bailiff stands over them to make sure they are working properly.

and carted home for so long that sometimes it is still out in the fields late in September, and sometimes much never gets carted home at all. The whole life of the village depends on a good harvest, and a bad harvest is sure to mean not getting enough to eat next winter. It may mean real famine, and perhaps famine sickness with it, so that many people will die of hunger and disease.

What John particularly dislikes is that on two or three days at haytime and two or three days at harvest he and all his family, except Alice, have to stop work on their own land to help Lord Robert to get in his hay and his corn. It is the same for every family in the village, serf or free, and John resents it bitterly. It is bad enough having to do compulsory work for the lord like a common serf. It is worse having to do it just when you are busiest on your own land, and it is worst of all in a year when the weather is bad, because Lord Robert has

The peasant and his neighbours are loading sheaves into the cart. The man on the left is tossing them in with a two-pronged pitch fork. Another, wearing his sun hat, is piling them up neatly in the cart. A third man holds the horse's head and keeps the animal quiet. The cart is very simple; only a wooden 'skeleton' really, and probably quite light enough for one horse. The wooden wheels are fixed on with a large peg or lynch pin, made of wood or metal.

the right to choose the days; sometimes he chooses the only fine days in a wet harvest, so that all the people in the village have to help get his crops in while their own are left to be ruined by the rain.

Assart land

When John can spare the time from his daily round of work on the land and his extra duties for his overlord, he works on his piece of assart land. This is his most valuable asset and the symbol of his free status and independence. Getting the land involved quite a complicated legal process for him and he had to ask for help from the lord's steward who has a sound knowledge of the law. First of all, John asked for permission to clear the land from Lord Robert, and paid him a money fine. In return Lord Robert, in the manor court in the presence of witnesses, gave him a charter granting him the right to clear so many acres of land in a precise place. He can grow what he likes, for his own profit, and he has the right to fence off the land so that no one may cross or use it without permission. The names of the witnesses were recorded in the charter and Lord Robert sealed it and gave it to John. He kept a copy of it on a roll of other grants and legal documents. This roll book is called a 'cartulary'.

Clearing the land is very hard work, for the trees must be chopped down by hand and the roots grubbed up and burned and all the weeds and scrub cleared before ploughing. John often comes to this work after a tiring day in the fields and can make only very slow progress. Sometimes he wonders if all the effort will be worth it, but when he feels like giving up he thinks of all the extra benefits it will bring eventually. It could be a worthwhile inheritance for his elder son and help to pay for Lambert's education if he wants to become a priest.

Clearing the assart before ploughing the new land. This man is using a crotched stick to hold the thistles while he chops them down.

far right: Digging the assart with a one-sided spade.

Serfs and craftsmen

The serfs

Other tenants on the estate are not so fortunate as John. Not all the freemen have the time and energy to clear assart land for themselves, and the serfs are more rigidly bound to the lord. They are not personally free, which means they are the lord's property and can be bought and sold like other goods. Serfs can be transferred to another estate or included in a grant of land. They must have the lord's permission to marry or to have their sons educated for the church. They cannot own or carry arms or take part in any official enquiry or be jury-men. They have to form groups of ten men (called 'tithings') to promise to obey the laws and, under the supervision of a leader, each one has to keep an eye on the others to make sure they do not break the law. If one of them does, the other nine must, on pain of punishment, bring him before the king's sheriff and accuse him publicly.

The serfs work on the land like freemen. Some of their time is spent on their own rented strips and some on the lord's land, and they have to help support the parish priest, too. Most of them pay one half to one third of their rent in cash and the rest in services, which are decided by the lord and recorded by his bailiff. Each duty has a money value, so that a serf holding land worth, for example, 8s a year, may pay the rent in 3s cash and the rest in different duties worth 3d or 4d each. The serfs do a fixed number of days' work each. Like the free tenants they plough, sow and reap, help with the harvests and work on the roads, but they also have to work in Lord Robert's garden and vineyard and help to plant, tend and harvest flax for his wife.

Typical of the wealthier serfs is John's neighbour Richard atte Field, who rents 18 acres of land for 7s 6d a year, payable on Lady Day (25 March), Midsummer's Day and Christmas. He also ploughs for the lord for six days a year—two days at the winter and Lent sowings and two days in the fallow fields, valued at 2d per day. He harrows for a day at both sowings (at 1d a day); mows the hay for four days in June (2d per day), and weeds the cornfields (½d per day). At harvest time he is obliged to reap for the lord at 2d per day and he may have to thresh, too. The cash value of all these services and the money rent Richard pays add up roughly to the same amount a freeman would pay in cash rent.

Richard atte Field, though unfree, is reasonably prosperous

This picture of a serf driving his pigs past a wattle fence comes from a modern film.

and does not have to give too many days of service to the lord. Some serfs have to give much more. William Godwyne has to do four days' work every week of the year. Besides this he has to give the lord a hen at Christmas and a basket of eggs at Easter. Others have to give grain at harvest; if they wish to buy or sell a horse they must first give Lord Robert 2*d*, and they have to pay him 1*d* for every pig and ½*d* for every piglet they own. The poorer serfs are the worst off, for they pay most of their rent in works and services.

A few of the unfree tenants hold their land by performing some special service. For example, Roger Cayleway holds a small plot in return for carrying important letters and documents for the abbot and the lord. Some tenants are women, holding their land in their own right and performing services in the same way as men. Agnes Hammod, another of John's neighbours, pays a cash rent of 21½*d* a year for her land and also digs the vineyard for three days (at 1½*d* per day) and gathers grapes for three days at the same rate.

Very occasionally a serf rises to an important position without gaining his personal freedom. In some places the manor reeve is a serf; he is the lord's personal agent and helps him manage the estate, collect the rents organise the manor

This picture of a man shearing sheep is taken from a twelfth-century English manuscript. The peasant has tied the sheep's legs together and is cutting fleece with metal shears, very like those still used today.

right: William the smith is shoeing the lord's horse, helped by his son and a boy. William himself is hammering in the nails with a big iron hammer which is forked on one side so he can pull out the nails of the old shoes. His son holds the horse's leg and the young boy holds the bridle and pats the horse to calm him during the shoeing.

The smith and his assistant are beating a piece of red-hot iron on the anvil. The smith holds the bar with a large tool, rather like pliers. Behind you can see the large pairs of bellows used to blow on the fire to keep it really hot.

court, keep accounts and records (with notched sticks if he cannot write) and generally see that things are running smoothly. He is allowed a cottage and land free of most normal rents and services.

A serf can gain his freedom in one of three ways. He can hope for generosity from his lord, but, although the church regards this as a great work of mercy, it rarely happens. The unfree man can save from his earnings and buy his freedom, if his lord agrees, or he can run away to a town for a year and a day without being caught, after which time he is free. If he is caught, he is brought back in disgrace and punished. By the 1200s, though, serfdom is already on the decline. Landholding has become much more complex and peasants, both free and unfree, are leasing and subletting land among themselves. It is often very difficult to establish a man's status and in the shire courts there are frequently cases involving serfs who claim to be free. Even lawyers cannot agree about the status of children with one free and one unfree parent.

Most serfs have little or no hope of becoming free men, and life can be very hard for them. In times of famine or unrest they are the first to suffer. If they poach or steal because they are hungry, the punishments are very severe and a man has to be really desperate before he will risk hanging or outlawry. In John's village, like others throughout the kingdom, some poor people die of hunger every winter and it is quite common to find their bodies at the roadside or in ditches. Though the priest tells them that they must be content with their life, for God appointed them to a particular place in society, the serfs are naturally envious of the richer freemen, like John, who have a chance to prosper and increase their property.

The craftsmen

The smallest group of tenants, mostly freemen, are the craftsmen, who pay money rents for their cottages, farm only enough land for their basic needs and spend most of their time on their own trade or craft. Most of them have some connection with farming, like the miller, blacksmith, thatcher and wheelwright. The blacksmith is the most important of all, for not only does he shoe horses and make farm implements; he also mends irons and pots, and makes weapons,

knives, chains, bolts and locks. Most peasant cottages are not worth locking, but the manor house has its treasures, like the lady's jewellery, the lord's weapons and the precious manor records. The church certainly needs a strong lock and iron hinges on its thick oak door. The smith buys his iron in the town from the ironmonger, who gets it from the smelter in the Forest of Dean in Gloucestershire.

The blacksmith has two sons, both of whom help their father. The eldest will probably take over when he is old enough, for it is usual for fathers to teach their sons their trade. Lambert likes to help, too, and loves to hold the horses' heads to keep them quiet while they are being shod. He sometimes thinks that he would like to be a smith himself, and if he is serious in this wish he will become an apprentice when he is older.

In John's village there is a carpenter and joiner, who makes ploughs, wooden spades, yokes for oxen and some furniture. John's kinsman is also a carpenter, but he specialises in buildings and helps to make the wooden frames, beams and rafters for cottages. When tenants build or repair their cottages they either ask for the carpenter to help them or borrow his tools and do the job themselves. They pay him in money or, more often, in goods such as eggs and grain.

Some villages have their own thatcher, but John's is too small to provide one man with full-time work, so a man comes over from a nearby village and stays for several weeks at a time to do all the work needed.

The craftsmen normally have more contact with the outside world, for they go to the town to buy materials or go to other villages to work, and they can bring all kinds of news from the town. They often buy interesting things for their families and friends. William, the smith, borrows John's cart for his trips to buy iron and nails, and brings back salt and cloth and, when times are really good, pepper and figs. Craftsmen can move to the towns and work there if they wish, but they often find the life hard and standards required of them high. Townsfolk are unwilling to let 'foreigners' in to work, and as there is always plenty to do in the country and the craftsmen have their own land and cottages, they are not generally keen to move.

A woman milking a cow which is tethered by a rope to a wooden post. The milk goes into a wooden bucket which has a handle to hold it steady. The cow is licking its calf.

Women

While John is at work on the land, his wife spends most of her time working hard herself. Like her husband, she gets up and goes to bed according to the sun. In winter the days are short and the family sleep longer, because it is expensive to burn lamps or candles, and they do not give enough light to sew or mend tools by. In summer, when the days are longer and warmer, the whole family gets up much earlier, not long after sunrise, and they rest at midday.

Alice gives John and her sons a breakfast of bread and ale and then tidies away the mattresses, which can be stored in the hayloft, or piled on top of the biggest chest. She has very little 'housework', as the cottage is so small, but she must

sweep the floor to clear away the bones and bits of food from the night before and put down rushes or straw on the floor to keep it clean and dry. She looks after the chickens, too, and feeds the birds with grain and household scraps. They generally scratch about in the garden by day, but at night they are shut away in the storeroom, to protect them from foxes and from thieves.

Baking and brewing

When John has taken his grain to be ground at one of the lord's two mills, he brings back the barrels or sacks of flour to his wife and she bakes it into coarse, dark rye bread. Her own cottage is not big enough to have a bread oven (though she can make flat cakes on a hot baking-stone by the fire) and

A man is taking a sack of grain to grind at the lord's water mill. A mule carries the heavy sack to the mill, where the grinding wheel is driven by the swift-flowing stream.

smus & asellus asdendo dictur. qi ase

so, like all her neighbours, she must use the lord's bakehouse up behind the manor house, where there is a huge oven. The village women take turns to bake large batches of loaves, carefully watched by one of the lord's servants who makes sure that each woman pays the proper fee – Lord Robert demands six loaves or a small sum of money every time the oven is used. Alice and her friends grumble about this a lot, but they know it is impossible to make bread at home so they have to do as the lord tells them.

Once every two or three weeks Alice brews beer. She used to have to brew it at the manor house and give Lord Robert some new ale as a fee, but now the new cottage is built there is room for John and Alice to brew and store their own beer. Because it is well known for its flavour and quality, Lord Robert still asks for a gallon or so at each brewing, and more at Christmas and harvest time, but now he pays Alice for it in cash, or, if she prefers, exchanges it for a small amount of pepper or spice. Most people drink a lot of beer as there isn't much else except water and milk. Sometimes women are allowed to sell the beer they have brewed and announce the fact by tying a branch or bush outside their houses. Before they are given permission to sell, the ale has to be sampled by the lord's reeve, or perhaps the abbot's bailiff, to make sure it is really good enough. They also decide on a fair price. It is a temporary privilege and does not give the seller the right to take guests or open her house as an inn. Every so often there are 'assizes of Bread and Ale' at the manor court, where both products are tested and people who dare to sell inferior or bad stuff are punished, usually with a fine or by being banned from selling.

Trips to the bakery and brewhouse, though hard work, are quite fun because Alice can see her neighbours and gossip with them. She also sees them when they go to the stream to wash clothes. Washing is very difficult for the ordinary women and often cold and unpleasant, because the only way to get things clean is to bang them on stone slabs by the stream and dry them over bushes and low branches. Some of the women have to get all their water from the stream, too, but John and Alice have their own small well, a great blessing and privilege.

Spinning and weaving

Apart from this work where she meets her neighbours, Alice spends most of her time at home and is very busy all day. When she has finished tidying and preparing meals, and making the cheese and butter, there is always plenty of spinning and weaving and sewing to do. Alice makes all her family's clothes herself from their home-produced wool. John has a few sheep of his own and most of the wool is sold to the abbot, but some comes straight from the shearing to Alice, who prepares it and makes it into rough 'homespun' clothes.

First of all, she cleans the raw wool with a 'card' – a piece of leather stuck with thorns or bits of wire, about the same shape and size as a handle-less hair brush. She combs it over and over to get out all the knots and impurities. Then she spins it, not on a wheel, but on the smaller, old-fashioned spindle or distaff, which she can tuck under her arm and carry about with her while she looks after the chickens or watches the pots on the fire or just gossips with her friends.

Then she weaves the thread into cloth on a small loom which

Carding the wool by hand before spinning. At the woman's feet is a basket with different cards.

A woman spinning with a distaff, from an early sixteenth-century drawing.

A picture from a life of Jesus (about A.D. 1300). We can see how cloth was dyed at home. The piece of cloth is hung over a bar suspended from the ceiling and let down into a large vat over the fire. The dyer pokes it down with a big wooden stick.

How to spin

1 Pull out and twist fibres.

2 Tie thread to spindle, looping round notch at top.

3 Twist spindle, so that twisting yarn runs back to intertwine fibres pulled from ball of fleece.

4 Keep spinning, stretching arm; see the picture on p.27.

5 Wind yarn on spindle; start again.

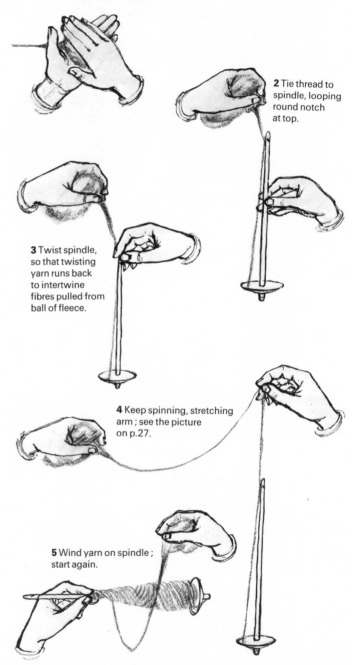

is kept in the storeroom and brought out into the main room and put close to the bigger window. Alice is part-owner of the loom. She shares it with her sister-in-law, because it cost a lot and is quite complicated to repair. After it has been woven, the cloth is trampled in water to shrink it and thicken it and make it warm. Then it is flattened with a hot iron and trimmed with huge metal shears and then Alice dyes it with water and vegetable dyes in a large pot. The most common colours are rather sludgy greens and browns and yellows. Really bright blues, reds and purples come from the expensive imported dyes which have to be bought in the town. Alice's cloth is warm and hardwearing and quite good enough for everyday clothes and cloaks and blankets, but when John has had a really good year, and the wheat has sold well, he can afford to buy pieces of extra fine cloth, professionally made, and Alice can make a gown for herself and tunics for John and the boys.

Alice is a kind and helpful woman, and when she can spare the time from looking after her own family she visits some of the old tenants in the village, people who are no longer able to work and who have to rely on the gifts of their generous neighbours to stay alive. One of these people is Alfred, son of Roger, who fought in the Crusades and tells Lambert wonderful stories of his adventures in the Holy Land, while Alice tidies up his tiny cottage and makes him some broth. She also visits sick neighbours and helps out when she can. In such a small village everyone knows everyone else and most people are friendly and helpful to those in need or trouble.

Children

The children are busy most of the time, too. There is no village school and most children have no formal education at all, though they are taught their prayers and the basic Christian beliefs by the parish priest. Some, if they are really keen, and their parents can afford it, can have lessons from the priest, either in the church, or, when it is too cold, in the priest's house nearby. Both John's sons have had that chance. Young John, nearly grown up now, learned to read and write, in English and very easy Latin, and to do accounts, but he was not really interested and much prefers to help his father on the land. John is willing to let him help as much as he can so that he can learn all about farming from experience. Already he ploughs and harrows his father's strips, helps to weed the fields and shear and stack the hay and corn at harvest. He is especially enthusiastic about clearing the assart and cultivating new crops there.

Young John will, he hopes, inherit his father's lands one day, but he would prefer Lord Robert to grant him some land of his own, when he is older. This could be done either by taking some of his father's lands and letting young John become the tenant, directly responsible to the lord and paying his own dues and services, or by accepting him as the heir of his childless uncle. Lord Robert could do either of these things if he wished. But all this is in the future and for the moment young John is content to work with his father and learn all he can.

Lambert, John's younger son, does not share his brother's ambitions. He enjoys his lessons with the priest far more and sometimes thinks that he would like to be a priest when he grows up. This would not be impossible as many of the ordinary parish clergy, including their own priest, Father Hugh, come from peasant families and began their education in the same way. If Lambert were really serious about entering the church he would first have to prove that he was freeborn. Then he would go to the cathedral school where he would study Latin, Theology, the Bible and the writings of famous Christian authors like St Augustine, and all about the ceremonies and services of the church, including singing and chanting. Then he would be carefully examined by the bishop and if he reached a satisfactory standard, and were old enough, he would be allowed to take holy orders and become a priest. Then a lord or bishop or abbot who was patron of a village church would present him to it as its priest.

Lambert knows that all this would be very hard work and that he would probably have to stay in the same parish for the rest of his life, since there is not much chance for a boy of humble birth to rise to important positions in the church. Still, he spends a lot of his time asking Father Hugh questions about his life and sometimes goes with the priest to visit the sick and poor in the village, to see all aspects of the priest's duties. He has not made up his mind definitely, as he is still very young.

When he is not with Father Hugh, Lambert works with his father and brother and runs errands for his mother, helping her to carry the flour to the bakehouse and the washing to the river. He sometimes has to help with the hens, which he hates. Lambert far prefers to work with his father's kinsman the blacksmith, because he loves horses. Sometimes he thinks he would like to be a blacksmith rather than a priest.

Both young John and Lambert love animals and they have all kinds of pets, including a puppy and an orphaned lamb. In spring they like to hunt for birds' nests and collect the eggs, and they have brought home several young birds with broken wings and tried to look after them. The boys help to look after John's two dogs and the other animals, and sometimes they go down to the manor house when Lord Robert and his friends are going hunting, to look at the beautiful horses and dogs and the specially trained hunting hawks. They are not allowed to hunt for themselves, but they can trap birds in large nets and fish in the village stream, with the lord's permission. Snaring rabbits is a favourite pastime, too, and a useful source of extra food for the family.

John and Alice had two other children, a boy and a girl who came between young John and Lambert in age, but they died young. It is very common for babies to die within a few weeks of birth because there are so many epidemics. Often there is just not enough to eat and children are born weak and sickly. Many children who do survive infancy live only to be about four or five years old, again because they are subject to all kinds of diseases, especially when a great sickness follows a hard winter or a time of famine. John and Alice were naturally sad to lose their other two children, but they accepted it as quite a normal thing.

The lord's wife is hunting duck with a hawk. She wears strong leather gloves to protect her hands and wrists. The man and the boy carry small drums.

Clothes

John's clothes are mostly made from woollen cloth.

His *hood* pulls down over his ears in winter.

His *shirt* may be made of wool or linen.

His *tunic* can be tucked up into his leather *belt* when he is working.

His *breeches*, under his tunic, are pulled tight by a draw cord at his waist.

His *stockings* may be gartered at the knee.

In the fields he may wear *boots*.

Alice wears her long hair in *plaits* and covers it with a *coif* or *veil*.

She wears a *gown* or *kirtle* of wool.

Under it is a *shift* of linen or wool.

Her woollen *stockings* are held by garters.

She wears leather *shoes*.

The villagers have to kill most of their cattle in the late autumn, because there is not enough to feed the cattle all through the winter. The meat will be salted and stored in barrels at home.

The lord's cooks are roasting duck and a pig on a spit before the fire. One turns the spit while the other piles more wood on the blaze. Whenever possible such cooking was done out-of-doors to lessen the danger of setting a wooden building on fire.

Amusements

Apart from church and church festivals and processions, the only real entertainment John and Alice and the children get is at Christmas and harvest time, when the lord gives them an entertainment and a feast. A visit to the manor house is always interesting. At Christmas time the great hall is decorated with branches of evergreen—fir, yew, holly, ivy and mistletoe. The fire in the central hearth is piled high with logs and the smoke swirls round the high rafters before going out of the great round hole in the roof. The fire gives some light and the hall is also lit by wooden torches, very carefully fixed in iron holders on the side beams of the walls.

On the raised platform at the far end of the hall sit the lord, his family, the priest and any special guests. The rest of the household and the villagers sit at long trestle tables down the hall. Christmas food is always better than at other meals; there are meat stews, ham and bacon and cheese and sweet-meats, and plenty of ale. The atmosphere is warm, cheerful and chaotic with everyone eating and shouting to servants, and children and dogs running about everywhere.

When the feasting is over the people are amused by jugglers and singers and sometimes by mummers, entertainers who wear masks and perform pantomimes. When the guests are tired and quieter, they tell stories. Most of them are old favourites which they all know and love—stories of the saints and their miracles; Saxon and Norse stories of the gods and heroes; French legends and the stories of King Arthur. Father Hugh knows some wonderful stories and will keep his audience attentive and spellbound for hours at a time. The older men are often willing to tell tales they heard from their fathers about the Crusades or the wars in France, and the people never get tired of hearing the adventures of old Thomas the pilgrim, who went all the way to the shrine of St James at Compostella in Spain and was shipwrecked on the way and captured by pirates. No one minds if the number of desperate pirates he killed increases at every telling; it is still a good story.

Sometimes at Christmas and harvest there is dancing and singing, too, and everyone can join in when the pipes (like our recorders) and drums are played. At harvest time the feast is usually outside in the courtyard on the village green. On other

The lord at high table. Notice the boar's head and the elaborately decorated jug and drinking bowl. He uses a sharp knife to cut his meat, but eats with his fingers. (From a calendar made about 1370.)

A Christmas feast. The lord sits at the high table, the more important guests sit at the table at his left and the villagers sit crammed together at the other 'low' table.

evenings there is little entertainment, apart from story-telling and playing dice, for the people haven't the time and skill to play chess and checkers like the lord and his family. When they do get time off, they are glad just to rest.

The children play all kinds of running and chasing games and, if they are allowed, hide and seek in the woods. Although most of them never go to school, they do not really have very much free time. They work hard for their parents, so they enjoy the feasts at the manor house, too, and are particularly fond of the stories.

Dancing at the Christmas feast.

2 CHURCH AND PEOPLE

The parish priest and his duties

Next to Lord Robert the most important and well-known person in the village is the parish priest, Father Hugh. He is of peasant stock himself – his father was a freeman on one of the abbey's estates – and the last abbot paid for his education and then appointed him priest (he has the right to choose the priest for all the parishes of the abbey's estates). Before he came to the village, Father Hugh had to promise the bishop and the abbot that he would live in the village permanently and do all his duties personally. He is not a scholarly man, but he knows enough to teach his people. Because he comes from a farming family himself, he can understand the village people's problems.

Father Hugh lives in a large cottage, worth 4 marks a year. It has several rooms, a loft, a garden and outbuildings. He lives with his servant and a housekeeper, his widowed sister. The priest's daily food comes from the common fields, for, like the other villagers, he has his strips although he does not work them himself. Instead he hires men to do the work for him. The servant sometimes helps out in the fields at harvest time, but he is mainly occupied with the priest's animals and bees and poultry. The sheep are penned with Lord Robert's and their wool is used for Father Hugh's clothes.

By right he can take one tenth of all the villagers' produce. This is called a 'tithe' and is generally offered in kind: wheat, rye, barley and oats, eggs, poultry, flour, fruit, bread and ale. It is stored in a special barn, called a 'tithe-barn', near the priest's house. He also keeps the money collected in church on certain days; for example, he may keep 2*d* at All Saints, 3*d* at Christmas, 1*d* for each burial, 1*d* for each christening, and whatever the people care to give when they come to Confession.

A tithe barn (Great Coxwell, Berkshire.) Father Hugh's barn would have been much smaller than this one, built for the monks of Beaulieu. The wooden framework is very like that of some manor houses.

30

Father Hugh's house

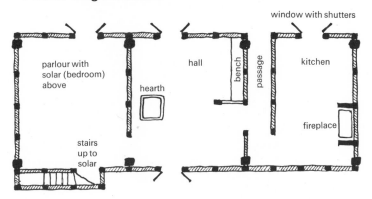

parlour with solar (bedroom) above

hall

window with shutters

bench

passage

kitchen

hearth

fireplace

stairs up to solar

The church building

The parish church is the most important and solid building in the village, because it is made of stone. There has been a church on the site since before the Norman Conquest. The old church, built in Saxon times, was made of wood and plaster, but as it was too small for the village, the people pulled it down in the middle of the twelfth century and replaced it with a handsome stone building. The 'new' church is in the Norman or 'Romanesque' style, with round arches and solid pillars.

The church is quite small, with a squat tower and one main door. In the arch over the door, and all round the windows on the outside, are carvings of animals, flowers and strange beasts, as well as the common zigzag and 'dog-tooth' patterns. Inside, the church has a nave and two side aisles, divided by stone pillars with pointed arches in the new style.

Inside, the arches and doorway are also decorated with

31

Kilpeck church, in Herefordshire, was built about the same time as that in John's village. You can see that it has round Norman arches and some later pointed ones. Kilpeck is one of the most richly decorated churches in the country, with strange beasts carved all around the doorway.

carvings. The wooden ceiling is painted in bright geometric patterns and the plastered walls are painted with scenes from the life of Christ and the miracles of the saints. The most interesting and impressive painting of all is over the main chancel arch, where all the people can see it – a representation of the Last Judgement or 'Doom'. It shows Jesus as judge, sitting in the centre; on his right hand angels lead the souls of the good up ladders to Heaven; on his left, devils push the wicked down to the flames of Hell. The villagers all know the meaning of this picture and the fate that awaits them if they do not live a Christian life.

There are many gilded and painted statues in the church, too; the most beautiful (and Alice's favourite) is the Virgin and Child which stands on the Lady altar in one of the aisles. Generally the services in the parish church are simple, but on special occasions, like Christmas and the feastday of the patron saint, there are processions and more candles and flowers and hymns. For a real spectacle, the people must go to the cathedral or the abbey church.

John's family and the church

Going to church

The church and the parish priest affect John's life at every stage. As a child he was taught his religion by the priest and, like all his neighbours, he was confirmed by the bishop. He goes to Mass on Sundays and feast days, to Confession and Holy Communion once a year at least, and says his prayers as he has been taught. He was married in the church porch and his wedding Mass was sung in the chancel; his two sons were baptised at the font and he knows that he will be buried in the churchyard nearby. He knows, too, that if he breaks the laws of the church and blasphemes, commits sacrilege or harms a cleric, he will be punished now and hereafter. The church also gives him entertainment, as his life can be rather dull and monotonous when there is little amusement, especially in winter. John finds the colour and beauty an escape from the drabness of his own surroundings.

John goes to Mass every Sunday and on the many feast days of the church. During the service most people stand or kneel as there are no seats. The very old or infirm may sit at the side on benches or on the low stone rims round the bottoms of the pillars, but most people have to do without a seat. Because he used to serve as an altar boy, John can understand some of the Latin of the Mass, but most people have no knowledge of the exact meaning of the words, and have to rely on the explanation given in English by the priest.

Father Hugh explains the Mass and other services to his people in English and teaches them the most important prayers in English and Latin. They learn them by heart and the main points are explained to them. In this way the ordinary people come to know the Lord's Prayer, the Creed, the Ten Commandments, the seven deadly sins and their opposite virtues, and the basic truths of their faith. Very few people can read and certainly no one, apart from Lord Robert and his family, can afford books, so everything has to be taught orally. Often, instead of a sermon, Father Hugh tells his people a story from the Gospels and explains it, so that they are familiar with the life of Christ and the parables.

The people have to come to Mass on important feast days, which are also holidays when there is no work. There are many such feast days, like Lady Day (25 March); St Peter and St Paul (29 June); Lammas (1 August); Michaelmas (the feast of St Michael and All Angels, 29 September) and All Saints' or All Hallows' Day (1 November).

St Christopher, patron saint of travellers. Many medieval churches had a wall painting of him on the wall opposite the main (south) door. Some people believed that if they caught a glimpse of the picture in the morning, they would be safe all day.

Father Hugh

The people help Father Hugh to clean and repair the church, for when the bishop comes round on a 'visitation' every few years, he not only has to see that the people are well taught and know their prayers, but he has to make sure that the church is in good repair. Father Hugh has to keep the lamps full of oil, the vestments and altar cloths mended and clean and the roof and windows repaired. The blacksmith helps to mend the huge iron hinges on the door and makes new iron candle holders, with spikes to fit the candles on.

They go to the parish priest for all kinds of help. Father Hugh visits the poor and sick and acts as a doctor, for he has some skill in simple medicine. The strange concoctions made by some of his parishioners are too much like spells and witchcraft for the priest's liking. Providing for the sick can be a great problem. The village is small and everyone knows everyone else; most people are related, so there is someone to look after those in need but often the people are too poor to help very much, however willing they might be. There are widows and orphans, too, who have little or no land and money and need help. Normally, the priest provides them with food and clothes from his own store or makes some kind of collection for them. Alice, as we have seen, often visits such people with food and John and his brother may help by cutting wood.

Father Hugh also helps out with problems over land-holding and rents and writes documents and letters for those who cannot write themselves.

The church's other uses

As the only 'public' building in the village where everyone can meet, the church is sometimes used for other things. Occasionally, the churchyard is used for celebrations on the feast of the patron saint, when the lord provides a feast for his people and everyone sings and dances far into the night. Father Hugh does not really approve of using the yard for such amusements but he cannot prevent them without permission from the bishop. Some villages and towns allow markets to be held in the churchyard, but fortunately the local bishop is strict and forbids such things. He is also very strict about animals in the churchyard and is glad to let Lord Robert and Father Hugh punish any peasant who lets his animals wander over church land.

Sometimes, the church is the scene of another kind of ceremony – if the lord frees one of his serfs. This must be done publicly, in the presence of the parish priest and king's sheriff. It must be recorded, with all the correct legal formulae, in official documents, and, above all, it must be seen to be done by as many people as possible, so that there will never be any doubt about the ex-serf's new status. The lord gives the newly-freed man his charter, with details of the rents and service he owes now, and a sword or spear to show that he is a freeman and able to bear arms. Sometimes this ceremony takes place in the shire court or hundred court, but when it is done in the village, everyone can join in the celebration. There was a great feast when Lord Robert freed Thomas atte Stream, a neighbour of John and his family. Freedom was given not only to Thomas, but to his wife, Hawisa, and his four children.

Other kinds of charters are granted in the church, too. Lord Robert gave one of his tenants the lands of a kinsman who had died of sickness and had no family. Lord Robert gave a copy of the charter to William the Red in the church porch, so that everyone would know that the strips of the dead Roger now belong to William, who pays $2s$ $4d$ a year for them.

In a nearby village the lord, Peter, gave the manor of Tettebury to Agnes his wife at the door of the church. John saw this ceremony, as he had to stop in Lord Peter's village while on his carting duties. He admired the newly built church there, with the new pointed arches and slender pillars.

3 LAW AND ORDER

The lord and life at the manor

John's overlord, Lord Robert Fitzralph, holds his land from the abbot. His main estates are in and around John's village, and his home, the manor house, is the centre of village life in some ways. He also holds land, worth a quarter of a knight's fee, in another part of the county; for this he pays a small cash rent to a neighbour and gives him a wreath of primroses every Easter and a wreath of roses every Midsummer's Day.

As lord of the manor, Robert Fitzralph is as busy as his tenants. He must see that his estate is kept in good order, that his tenants work hard and pay their rents and that every tenant is treated fairly. He has a large home farm which is managed for him by a bailiff. It is Lord Robert's duty to maintain law and order in the village and to deal with minor crimes and disturbances. He has to have a good knowledge of the law of the land, and to be able to understand legal documents and accounts. Unlike some of his neighbours, he can read and write, but he still needs the help of his steward and of the priest for more complicated matters.

Most of Lord Robert's time is taken up with the day-to-day running of the estate, but sometimes he has to do service directly for the king. Although he no longer has to serve as a knight for so many days a year, he still has certain obligations to the crown. For example, he must give evidence for tax and other financial enquiries and, as the most important inhabitant of the village, he is responsible for providing reliable information. Sometimes he will have to serve as one of the king's tax collectors. He may be asked to become a jury-man in the shire court, too. For all this work for the king he gets no pay.

The manor house

Naturally, Lord Robert's life is more comfortable than his tenants' in many ways. The manor house, where John and his family go with their neighbours at Christmas and harvest-time,

The lord and his wife. This illustration from a thirteenth-century book shows how cautious the lord had to be if he wanted to enlarge his estates by marriage; the circles below list all the relations (sisters, sisters' children, cousins, sisters-in-law etc.) that he might not marry.

is much bigger than the biggest peasant cottages and much more comfortable. It is built on the old Saxon pattern, with one main room (the 'Hall') which is used for eating, sleeping and all daily activities. It is built of wood and plaster and inside it the great wooden beams and rafters which support the roof are exposed. There is no fireplace or chimney and the fires, which are used for cooking, light and heating, burn in stone circles in the centre of the earth floor. The smoke escapes through a hole in the roof, just as in the cottages.

At meal times, trestle tables are put up and the lord and his family sit on a raised dais at one end of the hall, and their tenants and servants sit lower down on wooden benches. The servants sleep in the hall, too, on straw mattresses, but Lord Robert and his wife and children have two private rooms at

Not far from John's village, at Stokesay in Shropshire, a rich new lord built himself a particularly fine manor house of stone, about 1280. It still stands, though many small wooden buildings, like the kitchens, that stood in the courtyard have since disappeared. So has the moat that surrounded it. The half-timbered gatehouse in front was added three centuries later.

the end of the hall. Around the manor house are kitchens, storerooms, stables, barns and the communal bakehouse and brewhouse. Lord Robert also has a private garden, where his wife grows sweet-smelling flowers and herbs. There is also a vineyard and a piece of private ground where vegetables and flax are grown. Like his tenants, the lord keeps chickens

right: Here two of the lord's men are hunting a wild boar. The fierce animal is trampling one man, who is stabbing it with a hunting knife. The other man kills the beast with his spear. The poor dog seems to have been impaled on the boar's great tusk.

and bees and he also has a dovecote, with pigeons for fresh meat. (The picture above shows two pigeons in a dovecote.)

Everyday life at the manor

Lord Robert can afford to buy wine, spices and luxuries like silk and velvet for clothes for his wife and himself. Generally, though, they wear simple clothes like the peasants'; the material might be finer wool in prettier colours, but the basic everyday styles are the same.

For amusement, Lord Robert enjoys hunting, and John often sees him riding off with his friends to hunt deer on the abbot's land. Hawking is a favourite sport, too, and the ladies can join in. The hawks are very carefully trained to fly after ducks and small animals (see p. 26). They are expensive and Lord Robert is very proud of them. One of his tenants looks after them and it is almost a full-time job, for which he receives a small piece of land and a cottage. Other amusements are chess, checkers, singing, dancing and storytelling. Lord Robert also enjoys riding and fencing, which keep him in condition for fighting if he is ever called on to serve the king in some special campaign.

Lord Robert's wife is the daughter of another tenant of the abbey, a rich man who holds five knight's fees in all. When she married, the Lady Mathilda brought a 'dowry' of land

equal to a quarter of a knight's fee with her, and, in return, Lord Robert promised her a small house and piece of land on his other estate to support her in her widowhood, should he die first. The agreement was made publicly, before witnesses, and Lord Robert handed over the sealed legal documents to his wife in the village church in the presence of most of the tenants.

Lady Mathilda supervises the household and servants and sees to the running of the manor house. She is in charge of all the stores, including the wine-cellar, and oversees all the baking and brewing for her family. Like the peasant women, she spends much of her time spinning flax and wool for cloth. In the little spare time she has, she enjoys embroidery and makes fine belts and ribbons. If her husband ever had to go to war, she would make and decorate a 'surcoat' with his coat of arms on it to go over his chain mail. She also makes vestments for the parish church and for the abbey.

Though their life is easier than the peasants', it is not luxurious and they would be looked down on by the richer nobles, and even some of the wealthier townsfolks, for their simple dress and willingness to take part in household and farming concerns. Lord Robert, for example, is quite willing to help out at harvest alongside his tenants, and this would be frowned on by the higher nobility.

An extract from the manor court roll of the village of Tardebigge, Worcestershire. The records of the manor court of John's village would have been written out like this on a roll of parchment.

The audit

Twice a year, at Easter and Michaelmas, there is an audit, when Lord Robert does his accounts. All the tenants are called up to pay their rents and dues, and the bailiff is made to give all the particulars of all the money he has received and spent in running Lord Robert's home farm, down to the last farthing. This takes a long time, as every payment in money has to be counted and every payment in kind weighed out and checked, and all of them have to be written down by a clerk on a long parchment roll.

The manor court

One of Lord Robert's chief duties is to act as presiding judge in the manor court. As its name suggests, this court deals with purely local affairs which are too trifling to be taken to higher law-courts. The manor court meets several times a year and all the villagers are bound to come. In winter it meets in the hall of the manor house, and in summer, if it is fine, on the village green outside the church. Lord Robert presides over it and he sits with his steward (who can read and knows something of the law), Father Hugh and the parish clerk at a long table with parchment, quills and ink, ready to record all the cases, and a Gospel book from the church for swearing oaths.

Robert Fitzralph and a jury decide the cases according to local custom and the king's law. John often has to serve on the jury. Generally they do not now force an accused tenant to undergo trial 'by ordeal', the old way of testing a man's guilt or innocence by making him carry a red-hot iron or throwing him into the stream to sink or swim. If any villager is accused of a crime, he is brought before the court and publicly accused by the person or people he is supposed to have wronged. Both sides swear that they are telling the truth and bring witnesses to swear that they believe them. Accuser, accused and witnesses all take an oath on the Gospels to give true evidence. There is often no cross-examination and sometimes the man who can bring the most supporters wins the case, whether he is guilty or not; but usually the villagers have a pretty good idea of who is telling the truth and who isn't.

The cases, and their punishments, are carefully recorded by the lord's steward and the parish clerk. They are all simple and can be decided by the lord and the jury-men, with the advice of the other three. But one case has to be referred to a higher court. The smith found a stranger breaking into his forge in the act of stealing some of his tools, including a hammer and a sword he was repairing. He was caught red-handed and brought before the manor court. Lord Robert cannot deal with this case himself, as it is too serious and must be tried by one of the king's courts. Besides, the thief is not one of his tenants and seems to come from another part of the country. He decides to lock the accused man up securely in the manor house cellars until the king's sheriff next comes round, and then the smith can present his case to the hundred court. Lord Robert is relieved at not having to deal with the case himself, as it could be difficult, especially if the stranger is an outlaw and has no overlord, or if he is a condemned criminal on the run.

The meetings of the manor court are a pleasant change for the innocent. John enjoys the relief from the usual round of work on the land, although he does not like having to be a witness or jury-man. When the court's work is over, Lord Robert provides ale and bread for his tenants and a meal with wine for his three assistants.

Civil justice in the thirteenth century

The judges in the king's own courts at Westminster.

The justices in eyre who travel to hold assize courts in the main towns.

The king appoints the men who give judgement.

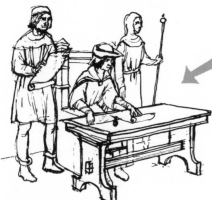

The sheriffs who hold shire courts and hundred courts.

Freemen serve as juries or sworn witnesses.

The lord of the manor with steward, priest and parish clerk.

Hawisa of Rowsley

Most of the cases are not complicated and are quickly settled, even one, more serious, case of disturbing the peace. Six villagers have banded together to complain about the shocking behaviour of Hawisa of Rowsley, who had a drunken brawl in her house late at night. She and her daughters and their guests were shouting and quarrelling far into the night and half the village heard them. Lord Robert and the jury-men deal very strictly with these rowdy women and they are all fined, not only for disturbing the peace late at night, but also for selling ale without permission and for daring to sell inferior ale. The bailiff and the lord tasted some of it and decided it was not good enough to sell. Hawisa and her daughters are banned from selling ale for three years and will have to let the bailiff inspect and sample every lot they brew from now on.

Hundred, shire and assize courts

There are three other kinds of civil court: the hundred court; the shire or county court; and the 'assizes', the most important of all.

The hundred courts

The hundred courts are still local but deal with a wider area than one village. Each county is subdivided into smaller areas which include several villages and the countryside around them. In the north, these areas are called 'wapentakes'; in Sussex, they are 'rapes' and in most of the rest of England they are 'hundreds'. Each hundred has its own court. Twice a year the king's sheriff judges serious crimes against the peace, like highway robbery and theft. The accused are 'presented' before the sheriff, as judge, in the same way as in the manor court, and each side brings sworn witnesses to support them. The sheriff usually deals with little misdeeds on the spot, but really serious crimes are left to the assizes and the accused person is locked up in the nearest castle or stronghold until then.

John and eight of his friends went to the hundred court one year to accuse a robber of attacking Edward by Brook, who was then acting as carter, on the high road, stealing his cartload of wine and salt and beating him severely with a cudgel. Luckily for Edward, some of the village children saw the whole incident and were able to run to fetch help. John and his friends rescued Edward and captured the culprit, an escaped thief on the run from another part of the hundred, and locked him up in Lord Robert's cellars. Then, when the sheriff came to the hundred court in the next village, Lord Robert and his servants brought the prisoner under guard before the court and John and the other witnesses gave testimony. The robber was ordered to appear before the king's judges at the next assizes, as this was too serious a crime for the sheriff to try. Besides he had committed several similar crimes.

The serfs from John's village have to go to the hundred court once a year, to see the sheriff in their 'tithing' groups. They have to register their names and groups and the sheriff has to check that each man belongs to a tithing.

The shire, or county court

The shire, or county court, as the name suggests, covers a whole county. The king's sheriff or 'shire reeve' summons the court and presides over it but the judges are a group of freemen of the county. It used to deal with disputes about land or inheritance, rents, dues and services, but now most of these are tried by the king's courts at Westminster, and the shire court deals chiefly with disputes about money or goods. The procedure is similar to that of the lesser courts; in the shire court, and in the hundred court as well, the sheriff gets a jury together – a group of twelve trusty local freemen who try to find out the facts of a case by questioning the people involved under oath and then presenting their evidence to the judge. There is no cross-examination and if a man is found with stolen goods on him or in his house or near a body, he is presumed guilty and punished. Punishments are much stricter than in the local courts and can be brutal. Trial by ordeal and by battle are sometimes used, but increasingly rarely.

Assize courts

Very occasionally, a case from John's village goes before the justices at Worcester. The king has specially appointed judges who go round their own area of England or 'circuit' (there are six such areas in the kingdom) hearing really serious cases which have been referred to them by the sheriffs. These 'justices in eyre' hold their 'assize' courts in the county towns. The sheriff summons the shire court to meet them, and they take it over and turn it into the king's assize court.

In John's area the assize courts are held at Worcester. The king's judges deal with the most serious crimes and also with the most complicated land cases. Once, when John was a boy, there was a murder case and, more recently, a body was found in a ditch near the village, but no one was found responsible for the death. The jury-men sent for witnesses and asked them questions, but no one could help them from John's village. More often, land cases are brought before the judges. One of Lord Robert's fellow tenants of the abbey brought an action against one of his neighbours about an acre of land and the house on it, and the legal expenses were very great because the plaintiff had to buy a writ (that is, a written order from the king to the sheriff) to bring the case before the assize judges, as the two parties involved served different lords.

John once went to the assize court at Worcester when he was in the city on an errand for his lord and he was very im-

A poor traveller being beaten and robbed on the high road. Detail from a manuscript picture.

pressed by the wisdom and knowledge of the king's judges. The whole court was much bigger and more crowded than the little manor court at home. John was rather frightened by all the clerks and judges in their robes and by the severe punishments given to real criminals, like robbers, forgers, murderers and people guilty of arson. Even though he has never committed a crime himself, he shudders when he remembers the number of men and women condemned to hang.

Church courts

Two other courts might affect John and his fellow tenants – the church courts and the king's forest courts. As the name suggests, the church courts are run by the church. In the bishop's court the bishop or his chancellor acts as judge, and the archdeacon holds a court as well. All cases concerned with marriage and wills are dealt with by these courts. For example, if there are any queries about inheritance or any disputes between heirs, then they take their case to the church's court. Bigamists and people pretending to be monks, nuns or priests are tried there, and so are all priests and other clergy who have done anything wrong. Some unscrupulous people claim to be priests because if they are caught committing a crime they will be tried in the church court, and punished less severely than in the king's court. The church courts also give special permission for things like the marriage of cousins and the remarriage of a widow who might have vowed never to marry immediately after the death of her husband. Anyone accused of blasphemy or swearing comes up before these courts, too.

King's forest courts

Much stricter, and greatly feared by John and all ordinary folk, are the king's forest courts. A great part of England is 'forest', that is specially protected wood and heath land where the king and his nobles can hunt. There are very strict laws enforced in the forests: no man may cut down trees or branches or gather wood; no man may light fires or damage the trees in any way. It is forbidden to bring dogs into the forest or to ride there and, of course, hunting or poaching is strictly forbidden. It is a great temptation for poor people to go into the forest at night to try to poach deer or birds, but if they are caught by one of the king's foresters or 'verderers' they are brought up before the forest court for that area and severely punished. Poachers might lose an ear or a hand and, if they are persistent offenders, they might be hanged. The forest judges are responsible directly to the king and the other judges have no authority over them. Dogs found wandering in the forest have their claws cut or their teeth drawn. People in John's village avoid the royal forest as much as possible and the children are strictly forbidden to go near it. Most people can remember the awful time when Alfred Thomson was caught poaching deer and was sentenced to lose his right hand. If John does feel like a little poaching – and he has only dared a few times – he will keep to the rabbits in the lord's woods and avoid the terrors of the royal forest.

The King's Bench was the highest court to which criminal cases could be referred. In the foreground warders guard the prisoners while at the top of the picture five judges in special caps and gowns are hearing a case. The prisoner stands with his counsel and a warder. Although the picture comes from the fifteenth century, the formal costumes may not have changed very much.

43

Visitors to the village

Life in John's village is steady and usually undisturbed by outside events. Occasionally, visitors from the outside world stray through and they arouse interest and curiosity and, sometimes, alarm among the people. A most unwelcome intruder is the pursued criminal, chased by men from the next hundred. It is the villagers' duty to chase and catch him, though they usually let him go on to the next place and try desperately to prevent him from running into the church for sanctuary.

Others are more welcome. There are sometimes pilgrims on their way to Worcester or St Winifred's Well, and they have wonderful travellers' tales to tell about their journeys and the things they have seen, like miracles of healing at the tomb of St Thomas at Canterbury Cathedral. There are soldiers going for garrison duty in local castles and they can tell hair-raising stories of wars in France and battles with the Welsh on the borders. Beggars and vagabonds are quite common, too, and they tell hard-luck stories to wheedle money out of the soft-hearted. Most popular of all are the pedlars, who bring all kinds of pleasant things in their packs, like coloured silk thread, wools for embroidery, braid, brooches, buckles, spoons and knives. The pedlars are usually on their way to one of the fairs or markets in the towns but they find the diversion worthwhile. Alice bought a pretty pair of buckles and some spoons from the last travelling salesman who came.

There are more frequent and regular visitors who cause little curiosity because the people know them. The abbot's reeves pass through the village now and then on their way to some of the abbot's estates where he farms his own land. They are especially busy and active around sheep-shearing and harvest, when they stay on the abbot's sheep farms for days at a time to help supervise work. Though they are busy men, they are quite willing to stop and discuss prices with

King's officials collecting and weighing coins. The sheriff of each county collected the taxes and took them twice yearly to the king's exchequer, where they were counted and weighed. £1 worth of silver coins was supposed to weigh 1 lb, and if the coins were underweight, because of clipping, the sheriffs were punished.

John and his friends and to pass on any important news from the outside world. They travel round all the abbey's estates, which are scattered round the west midlands and the Cotswolds, and pick up all kinds of titbits of news about the king's wars and politics in general.

Less popular and, luckily, less frequent visitors are the king's clerks. From time to time there is a great official enquiry into law and justice and the king's clerks come round to hear complaints against sheriffs or justices. The evidence is always given on oath and always written down with the help of the lord and of the priest. Most villagers are wary of these royal clerks and are hesitant to give information but they have no choice, and Lord Robert explains that it is for their own good in the long run.

A trip to town

Sometimes, on treasured and glorious occasions, John gets the chance to travel on his own, as carter for his lord. Many of his friends find this service a bore and a nuisance but John looks forward to it eagerly. Carting is a duty only given to free peasants with a horse, ox or mule and cart, and as John has a strong wooden cart and his brother has two horses they are sometimes chosen.

Lord Robert has a large farm, and every year after harvest he has a lot of corn to sell. The abbey has many monks and servants to feed, and every year it buys some of Lord Robert's corn. The carter who carts the corn to the abbey also does errands for Lord Robert before he comes back.

One year, John went first to the abbey with corn, then he was sent to Worcester to buy spices, wine and cloth, and then he went to a cell of the abbey to deliver some more of his lord's corn. (A cell is a small house of monks which belongs to the main abbey.) Then he went home again with the wine and other things, having enjoyed himself and met all kinds of interesting people on the road.

The journey

This year John has to make a similar trip, with a cartload of grain and two tuns of ale. He takes with him his younger son Lambert for company and one of their dogs to guard the cart. Alice has given them bread, cheese, apples and pears, and ale in leather bottles.

They reckon on a journey of a week or so and take money with them for food and lodging and for buying cloth, salt and iron in the town. John knows that the cart will be half-empty on the last stage of the trip, so he hopes to load it up with goods for his family and neighbours. All their money is safe in a strong leather purse which John keeps on his belt, and in case of attack he carries a wooden pole and a knife.

The road out of the village is quiet enough, and they pass only a few neighbours filling up pot-holes before the winter rains. The corn has all been gathered in and the animals are feeding peacefully in the two great fields. John and Lambert go on until nearly nightfall, when they stop at the cottage of a wheelwright who is one of Alice's cousins. He and his wife give them a warm welcome and supper and a bed for the night.

The next day they start off early and pass long trains of pack-horses and mules, all laden with sacks of wool, going to Bristol or Gloucester. Further on, they are passed by an important-looking pair of men dressed in black and attended by many servants and clerks. They have several baggage carts and seem rich and powerful. A hedge-cutter tells John that they are the king's judges going to the assize courts at Worcester.

They also pass a clergyman in a habit (or dress) they have not seen before – a white robe with a long black cloak and hood. Lambert decides to ask the guest master at the abbey what order this strange monk belongs to. After another day's

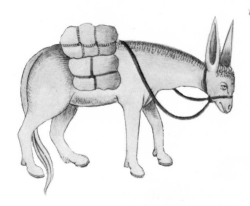

A pack-mule laden with sacks of wool.

Dominican friar.

Only rich people could afford to travel in a carriage like this (from a fourteenth-century drawing).

journey they reach the abbey gateway and the porter comes out to greet them and to ask their business. They are shown to the farm buildings and barns and are met by the steward, who is not a monk, but a paid employee of the abbey. He checks the sacks and tuns, records the amounts on his parchment, and then sees that the horses are stabled by his assistant.

The stay at the abbey

John and Lambert, like all visitors to the abbey, are cared for by the guest master, the monk in charge of hospitality in the special 'guest house' apart from the main abbey buildings. After a short prayer of thanksgiving for a safe journey, the two are shown into the guest house, where they are given supper. The guest master stays with them for a while and explains that the strange monk Lambert saw was not a monk at all, nor a priest, but a friar of the Order of St Dominic, the 'Black Friars' (so called because of their black cloaks), who have recently come to England from France and are founding houses all over the south and midlands. They do not live in

a monastery all the time, but serve God by wandering from place to place, preaching and doing good wherever they are needed.

The town of Worcester

John has to go to Worcester to buy wine and sugar for Lord Robert and he has been given enough for a night's lodging on the way. At Worcester, he and Lambert will stay in a religious house. After another two days they reach the city and leave the horse and cart at the appointed stable and go in search of the wine merchant. He is rich and proud but his foreman is friendly enough; he tells them that the tuns of wine are already ordered and paid for and promises to bring them to the stables.

The foreman is quite willing to answer Lambert's eager questions about where the wine comes from and how it is transported. This wine is from Gascony, a part of western France still under the rule of the king of England, and has been exported from Bordeaux to Bristol and then brought to Worcester and other towns in the west and midlands. Loading

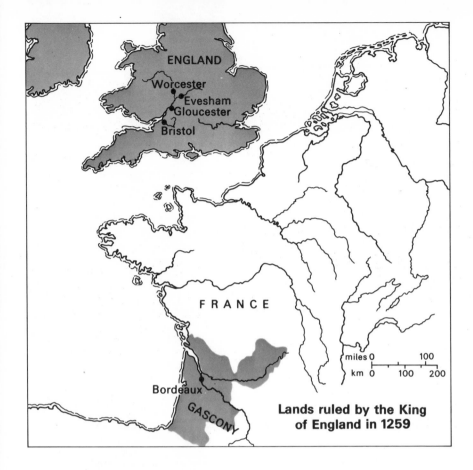

Two French coins (*gros tournois*) minted in the reign of Louis IX and introduced into circulation about 1258. Lambert's coin may have looked like one of these.

the tuns takes quite a long time, but there is still time left over to buy iron bars for the smith, salt for several neighbours and for Alice and a piece of purple cloth to make a dress. Lambert is fascinated by the merchants' houses and showrooms, which are much bigger than anything he has seen at home. He is also delighted with the French coin that the friendly foreman gave him when they left the wine-merchant's.

John and Lambert spend the night in Worcester and set off again after early Mass. They go to the cathedral, partly to pray for a safe journey home and partly to show Lambert the beautiful building and the grave of King John, the present king's father. Then they go back to the abbey to deliver the tuns of wine, and from there home again, stopping to deliver salt and salt-fish at the wheelwright's cottage.

Coming home

After eight days away from home, they return to the village, very pleased with their trip and all the things they have seen and done. Alice is delighted with the cloth and she cooks them a special supper. Lambert has a good deal to talk about and remember. He is eager to show the coin to his brother, but when he sees his own village and the familiar church and cottages and smells the fresh air and hears the sounds of the dogs and sheep and church bells, he is glad to come back to the country. John feels the same; the town is exciting, it is wonderful to travel and not have to work on the land for a week or so, but country life is what suits him and his village is where he belongs.

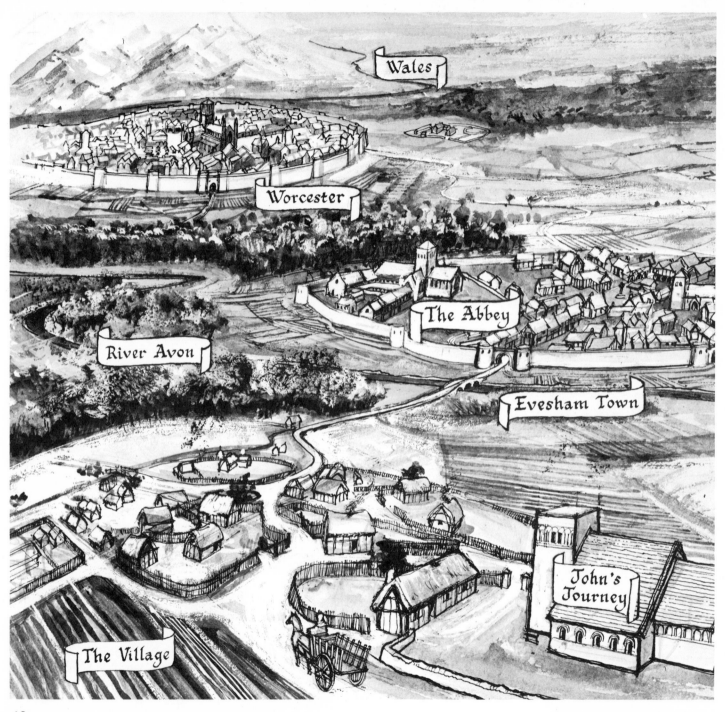

Wales

Worcester

The Abbey

River Avon

Evesham Town

John's Journey

The Village

Index

Acknowledgments

Most of the illustrations in this book are taken from manuscripts written and illustrated in the Middle Ages, usually about the period that is described in the book. These manuscripts are now in the three libraries listed below, and the pictures are used by kind permission of the respective libraries. The manuscript reference is given first, then, in parentheses, the page references for the pictures in this book.

The following manuscripts are from the Bodleian Library, Oxford: Ms. Corpus Christi Coll. 285, 13th-century choir psalter, ff. 3v (p. 11, fire), 6v (p. 13), courtesy the President and Fellows of Corpus Christi College, Oxford; Ms. Douce 88, 13th-century treatise, ff. 51 (p. 21), 111v (p. 11, bees); Ms. e.Mus. 136, f. 6v (p. 14); Ms. Rawl. D.939, 1370 calendar, Sect. 2 (p. 15, sowing, p. 18, clearing), Sect. 3 (p. 15, tools, p. 28, slaughtering, p. 29, lord); Ms. Add. A.46, 13th-century calendar, f. 4v (p. 16); Ms. Selden Supra 38, ff. 21 (p. 17), 27 (p. 24, dyeing); Ms. University Coll. 100, f. 57 (p. 17, harvesting); Ms. Douce 104, f. 39 (p. 18, digging); Ms. Auct. D.2.6, 12th-century St Albans calendar, f. 4 (p. 19); Ms. Bodley 764, 13th-century bestiary, ff. 38v (p. 38, boar), 41v (p. 22), 44 (pp. 23, 26), 80 (p. 38, dovecote); Ms. Ashmole 1504, English herbal, ff. 30 (p. 45), 34 (p. 24, spinning); Ms. Auct. D.3.2, 13th-century Bible, f. 238 (p. 29, dancing); Ms. Rawl.A. 384, f. 91 (p. 36); Ms. Douce 131, 14th-century psalter, f. 43 (p. 46).

From the British Library: Sloane Ms. 3938, f. 5 (p. 20); Roy Ms. 10.Eiv, f. 138 (p. 24, carding); Ms. Add. 42130, Luttrell Psalter, f. 206v (p. 28, roasting); Ms. Egerton 1894, f. 20v (p. 29, table).

From the Cambridge University Library: Ms. Ee.3.59, f. 4r (p. 42); Trinity College Ms. R.17.1, f. 230r (p. 44).

The author and publisher would also like to thank the following for permission to reproduce illustrations: p. 5 Department of Aerial Photography, University of Cambridge; p. 8 National Buildings Record; p. 11 (cauldron and pots) Museum of Archaeology and Ethnology, University of Cambridge; p. 12 Mr J. Higgs; p. 13 (plough) Mr T. Corfe; p. 19 (pigs) from a Gateway Productions film *Medieval Society*; p. 30 Edwin Smith; pp. 32, 34 National Monuments Record; p. 37 Aerofilms Ltd; p. 39 County Council of Hereford and Worcester; p. 43 Cambridge University Library; p. 47 Syndics of the Fitzwilliam Museum, Cambridge.

This picture of a man shearing sheep is taken from a twelfth-century English manuscript.

Drawings by Valerie Bell

front cover: John and his family prepare for ploughing. This picture by a modern artist shows the family described in the book and their home.
back cover: This picture of the imaginary village described in the book is based on the remains of the deserted village shown in the air photograph on page 5.

The Cambridge History Library

The Cambridge Introduction to History
Written by Trevor Cairns

The Cambridge Topic Books
General Editor Trevor Cairns

The Cambridge History Library will be expanded in the future to include additional volumes. Lerner Publications Company is pleased to participate in making this excellent series of books available to a wide audience of readers.

Lerner Publications Company
241 First Avenue North, Minneapolis, Minnesota 55401